Creative Clarinet Duets

26 stylish duets for beginners

Kellie Santin

Cheryl Clark

OXFORD
UNIVERSITY PRESS

T0088406

Dear Student,

Creative Clarinet Duets is a fabulous collection of 26 stylish duets that encourage beginner students to enjoy making music with other players both inside and outside of lessons. It is intended to be used alongside the first book in the series, *Creative Clarinet,* and the duets follow the progression of that book. There are helpful references to the corresponding chapters at the start of each piece.

All of the duets have their own backing track included on an accompanying CD. These offer the player an authentic experience of performing within an ensemble.

This is the second book in the *Creative Clarinet* series and it is followed by a third, *Creative Clarinet Improvising,* which expands on the skills introduced in books one and two.

Thank you for choosing *Creative Clarinet Duets.* We wish you many hours of happy music making!

Kellie Santin   Cheryl Clark

Contents

Creative
Clarinet
Duets

Title	Creative Clarinet Chapters	Page	Track
Let's go	1–3	5	1
Equality	1–3	5	2
Taking it to the limit	1–3	6	3
Blast from the past	1–3	6	4
Mind the gap	1–5	7	5
Two's company	1–5	7	6
Jet lag	1–5	8	7
Cutting edge	1–5	8	8
Craving calypso	1–8	9	9
It's an illusion	1–8	10	10
Elizabeth	1–10	11	11
Put on your red shoes	1–10	12	12
The happening thing	1–10	13	13
Secret agent shuffle	1–13	14	14
Anyone for tennis?	1–13	15	15
In the meantime	1–13	16	16
Empty cupboards	1–15	17	17
Moving right along	1–15	18	18
Squeaky clean	1–15	19	19
Never say never	1–18	20	20
Excess baggage	1–18	22	21
Cool bananas	1–20	24	22
Under cover	1–23	26	23
Hot off the press	1–23	28	24
Gone troppo	1–25	30	25
And the winner is . . .	1–25	32	26

A tuning note (B) is located on track 27

Playing along with the CD

♫ Tune up using the tuning note located on track **27**. The tuning note is **B**.

♫ Both parts are played on the CD. The top line is found on the left channel, and the bottom line is found on the right channel.

♫ When you are confident at playing your part, pan left or right (using the balance control on your audio equipment) and mute the part that you are playing. In this way, you can play along with either part as a duet.

♫ Remember to listen closely to the count-in at the beginning of each tune.

♫ Count the rests accurately.

♫ Most importantly, HAVE A GREAT TIME!

Chapters 1–3

① Let's go

Kellie Santin

Chapters 1–3

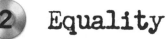
② Equality

Kellie Santin

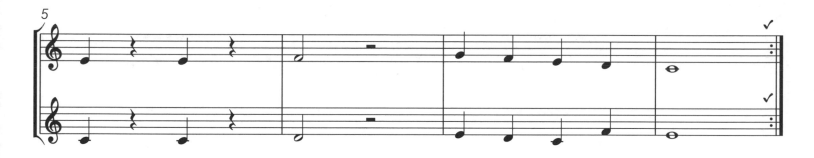

3 Taking it to the limit

Cheryl Clark

4 Blast from the past

Cheryl Clark

Chapters 1–5

5 Mind the gap

Kellie Santin

Chapters 1–5

6 Two's company

Kellie Santin

Creative Clarinet Duets

Chapters 1–5

7 Jet lag

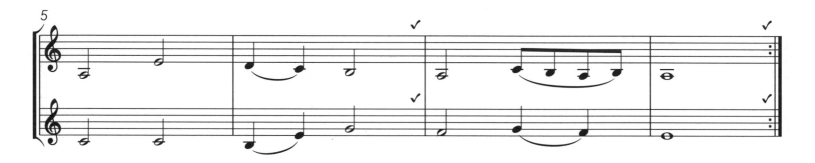

Chapters 1–5

8 Cutting edge

Chapters 1–8

9 Craving calypso

Kellie Santin

Chapters 1–8

10 It's an illusion

Cheryl Clark

Chapters 1–10

 Elizabeth

Kellie Santin

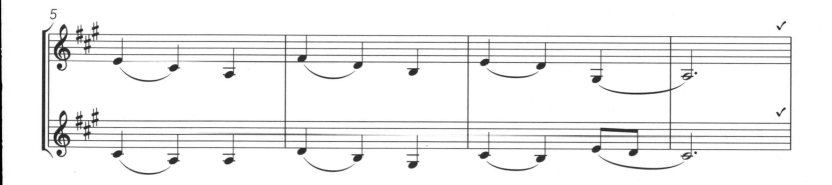

Creative Clarinet Duets

12 Put on your red shoes

Cheryl Clark

Latin

Chapters 1–10

13 The happening thing

Cheryl Clark

Creative
Clarinet
Duets

14 Secret agent shuffle

Kellie Santin

Shuffle

Chapters 1–13

15 Anyone for tennis?

Cheryl Clark

Creative Clarinet Duets

16 In the meantime

Kellie Santin

Rock

Chapters 1–15

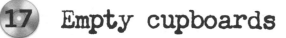

Empty cupboards

Kellie Santin

Slow Blues

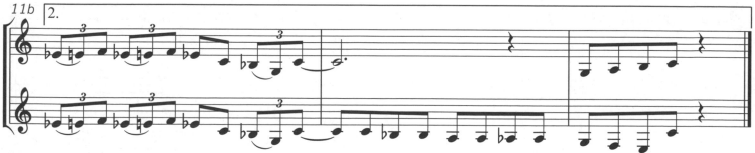

Creative Clarinet Duets

Chapters 1–15

18 Moving right along

Cheryl Clark

Chapters 1–15

 Squeaky clean

Cheryl Clark

Chapters 1–18

20 **Never say never**

Kellie Santin

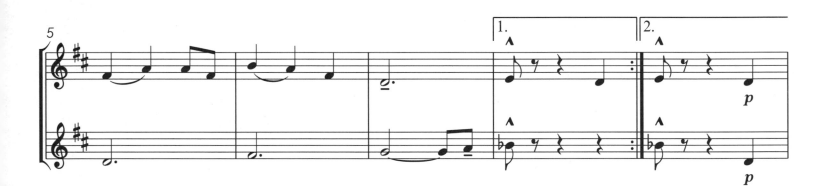

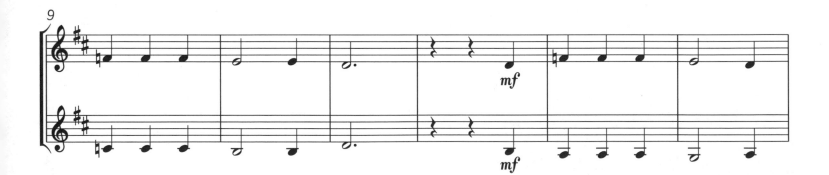

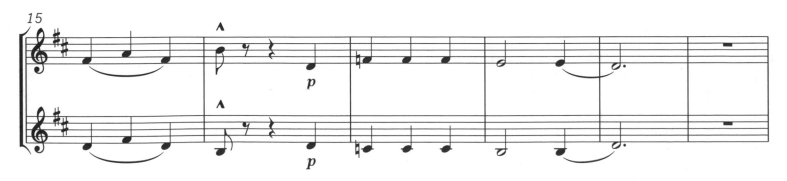

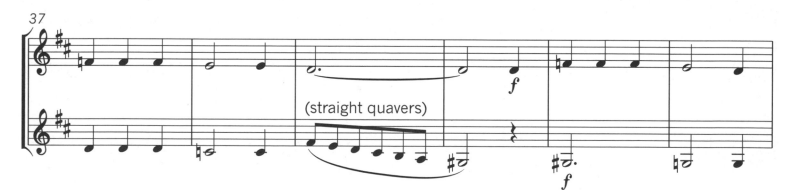

Creative Clarinet Duets

21 Excess baggage

Kellie Santin

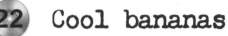 **Cool bananas**

Cheryl Clark

Latin

Creative Clarinet Duets

23 Under cover

Kellie Santin

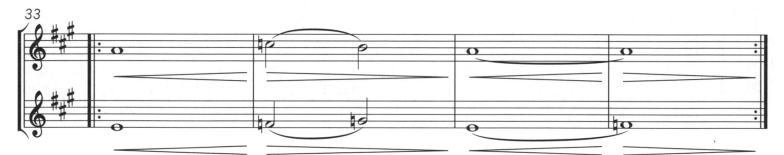

Creative
Clarinet
Duets

Chapters 1–23

24 Hot off the press

Cheryl Clark

Jazz Waltz

Creative Clarinet Duets

 25 Gone troppo

Cheryl Clark

Fast Latin

mf (1st time)
f (2nd time)

mf (1st time)
f (2nd time)

Creative Clarinet Duets

31

Creative Clarinet Duets

26 And the winner is . . . .

Kellie Santin

Fast Rock

Fine   D.C. al Fine